IMAGES OF WAR

VICTORY IN THE PACIFIC & THE FAR EAST

RARE PHOTOGRAPHS FROM WARTIME ARCHIVES

ANDY RAWSON

Pen & Sword
MILITARY

First published in Great Britain in 2005 by
PEN & SWORD MILITARY
an imprint of
Pen & Sword Books Ltd,
47 Church Street, Barnsley,
South Yorkshire.
S70 2AS

Copyright © Andrew Rawson, 2005

ISBN 1-84415-289-8

The right of Andrew Rawson to be identified as Author of this
Work has been asserted by him in accordance with the
Copyright, Designs and Patents Act 1988.

A CIP catalogue record for this book is available from the
British Library

*All rights reserved. No part of this book may be reproduced or
transmitted in any form or by any means, electronic or mechanical
including photocopying, recording or by any information storage and
retrieval system, without permission from the Publisher in writing.*

Designed and typeset (in 12pt Gill Sans Light)
by Sylvia Menzies, Pen & Sword Books Ltd

Printed and bound in Great Britain by CPI UK

Many of the photographs in this book have been reproduced
with kind permission of the United States National Archives.
Captions indicate the photograph reference number.

Pen & Sword Books Ltd incorporates the imprints of
Pen & Sword Aviation, Pen & Sword Maritime, Pen & Sword
Military, Pen & Sword Select, Pen & Sword Military Classics
Leo Cooper and Wharncliffe Local History

For a complete list of Pen & Sword titles please contact:
PEN & SWORD BOOKS LIMITED
47 Church Street, Barnsley, South Yorkshire, S70 2AS, England.
E-mail: enquiries@pen-and-sword.co.uk
Website: www.pen-and-sword.co.uk

Contents

Introduction by the Author

After the surprise attacks on Pearl Harbour and the Philippines in December 1941 and the fall of Singapore the following spring, the Allies had been on the defensive in the Pacific and the Far East. Following naval victories and bloody battles as far apart as Tarawa in the Pacific and Kohima in India, the Allies were ready to strike back.

The tide turned in the autumn of 1944 as British and Indian troops made progress through the jungles of Burma while Chinese troops, with the help of American supplies and equipment, held the Japanese at bay.

The Americans struck back in the Philippines in December 1944, heralding the start of a six month campaign to clear the chain of islands, allowing General MacArthur to fulfil his promise to return. The capital, Manila on the main island of Luzon, was captured in March 1945 but resistance across the islands continued through the summer as the Japanese chose to fight in the jungles and mountains rather than surrender.

The US Marine Corps landed on Iwo Jima, an isolated volcanic island halfway between Saipan and Tokyo, in February 1945. After landing under withering fire, the Marines conquered Mount Suribachi, leaving one of the endearing images of the Second World War, the raising of the Stars and Stripes on the summit. Fierce fighting continued for over a month with horrendous casualties on both sides; over 45,000 men were killed or injured on the tiny island. Once the island had been cleared, Tokyo no longer had an early warning radar station against bombing raids, and the Americans had a new airbase to launch devastating air raids on the Japanese homeland.

Okinawa, the gateway to Japan, was next; the Americans needed the island as a staging area for the final attack on the Japanese mainland. The landing, codenamed Operation ICEBERG, at the beginning of April, was unopposed, but the Japanese were waiting inland hiding in hills they had spent months fortifying. Again, there was bitter fighting as the Americans resorted to blowtorch and corkscrew methods to blast or burn the Japanese out of their tunnels, but as American casualties soared to over 35,000, the Japanese leader realised he had been beaten, and committed ritual suicide, many of his men followed his example or fled into the hills.

In Burma, the British continued to put pressure on the Japanese, and, after crossing the Irrawaddy River in April 1945, raced south to the capital Rangoon, while Chinese troops went over to the offensive. With the tide turning against them on all sides, the Japanese were forced to withdraw into Thailand and await their fate.

The fighting across Burma and the Pacific was brutal, as the Japanese resorted to suicidal tactics and the Allies unleashed every type of weapon available to them. Planes, ships, artillery, tanks, flamethrowers failed to subdue the Japanese and the Americans had to eventually resort to a fearsome new weapon – the atomic bomb. Two were dropped on Hiroshima and Nagasaki at the beginning of August, and within days, the Japanese were suing for peace. Over 250,000 civilians were killed, and thousands more suffered for years to come from radiation sickness, but Operation OLYMPIC, the projected invasion of Japan, would not have to be launched. The conclusion of the war in the Pacific had heralded the start of the nuclear age.

Chapter One

Burma and China

The Japanese attempt to take Imphal, the gateway to India, had stalled at Kohima in the spring monsoons of 1944. General William Slim's Burma Corps, composed of British and Indian troops, held back General Mutaguchi's divisions in fierce fighting and by July the Japanese had to fall back starving and low on ammunition.

British Fourteenth Army followed through the rain soaked jungle and crossed the Chindwin at the end of November but Vice-Admiral Lord Louis Mountbatten, the commanding officer of South East Asia, was forced to divert troops and supplies elsewhere, allowing the Japanese to withdraw across the Shwebo Plain and behind the Irrawaddy River under their new commander General Hyotaro Kimura.

With only four infantry divisions, two tank brigades and a minimum of air support under his command, Slim opted to make a feint crossing near Mandalay while IV Corps attacked at Nyaungu, 100 miles downstream. During the early hours of 14 February the Japanese were alerted as the leading wave sailed across the wide river and the British and Ghurkha troops suffered heavy losses. Tanks gave covering fire at first light and Indian troops crossed to secure a slender hold on the far bank. With a bridgehead secured, IV Corps could advance across the Burma Plain to Meiktila, the Japanese communications centre in Burma.

Fighting side-by-side, the British and Indian soldiers encountered fanatical, and at times suicidal, resistance but still entered the town on 6 March, forcing the majority of the garrison to retire while a rearguard held on, at the ancient Fort Dufferin until the 21st, and only surrendered after bombers had blasted holes in the fortifications. With the monsoon season about to begin, Slim ordered XXXIII Corps to focus the Japanese attention along the Irrawaddy River as IV Corps advanced on a narrow front down the Sittang River. It was a risky operation but the gamble paid off and by 23 April they had advanced over 300 miles, capturing Toungoo as Tokyo ordered a general withdrawal to the coast in response to American successes in the Pacific.

While IV Corps struck deep into the heart of Burma, XV Corps had progressed with Operation DRACULA, a series of amphibious landings along the west coast. An attack on the Arakan area in December 1944 had been followed by the capture of the port facilities at Akyab and the airfields on Ramree Island a month later. By the end of April Slim was ready to launch the final attack against Rangoon, and on 2 May, Indian paratroopers landed south of the city while 26th Indian Division came ashore on both sides of the Rangoon River. The city was deserted; the Japanese had

The Allied Air Forces relentlessly pounded the Japanese supply lines, targeting bridges, roads and camps as they fell back towards the Chinwin River. This RAF Hurri-bomber is making a low level bombing run against a bridge on the Tiddim Road.

withdrawn and the local population turned out in force to cheer the Indian troops as they moved into the heart of the city.

600,000 men of General Kimura's army had withdrawn across the Sittang River into the flooded paddy fields and grasslands along the Thailand border. Starving and low on ammunition they fought on until they were killed or died from malnutrition or disease. Finally, on 4 August, Mountbatten was able to announce that Japanese resistance had ended, drawing to a close the bitter campaign in the mountains and jungles of Burma.

While General Slim fought with the Fifteenth Army in Burma, Generalissimo Chiang Kai-shek and his American adviser, General Vinegar Joe Stilwell, were trying to stem Japanese ambitions in China. Despite Stilwell's advice and American aid, the Chinese divisions were poorly trained and the Japanese spring offensive of 1944, Operation ICHI-GO, had easily overrun the Peking-Canton railway. Only the monsoons saved General Chiang's men and by the autumn the Japanese had exhausted their supplies near their final objective, the American airfields around Chungking.

In China's Yunnan province, twelve inadequately equipped divisions of China's Y-Force had been on the counter-offensive since May but had made little headway against the organised Japanese. Although disorganized, Chinese troops supported, by the Fourteenth US Air Force, engaged a million Japanese soldiers, losing over 700,000 casualties as they halted their offensives at Lungchow and along the Canton-Hengchow railway.

When General Albert Wedemeyer replaced Stilwell in October 1944, American and Chinese relations started to improve and Chiang Kai-shek agreed to stop relying on the American bombers and rebuild his army so he could start to fight back. The new alliance worked and as Y-Force advanced beyond Tengyueh and Lungling, the Chinese conscripts began to drive back the Japanese.

After being on the defensive for over three years, at long last the British Fourteenth Army could go on the offensive. This Lee-Grant tank assisted 5th Indian Division during the attack on the Japanese positions around Tiddim.

January 1945 was an important turning point in China as Chiang's two Armies met and the first convoy drove along the Ledo Road. Work had started on the supply route as early as December 1942 and for two years 80,000 American engineers and Chinese labourers battled the weather and terrain to push a single-track road over mountains, through jungles and along narrow gorges. The British thought it was a folly as the lorries would consume vital fuel to carry the supplies but General Stilwell was anxious to appease the Chinese and a 1,800-mile long fuel pipeline connecting Calcutta and Kunming alleviated the problem. The material effect might have been questionable but the boost to Chinese morale was incalculable. Although Chiang had never seen eye-to-eye with Stilwell, he named the road in honour of his vitriolic advisor.

A final Japanese attack in March 1945 captured the American air base at Laohokow but an attempt to capture the air base at Chihkiang failed: it was the first Japanese setback. The Chinese struck back, driving their exhausted and starving enemy before them. On 9 May, as the Soviet Union prepared to declare war, Tokyo withdrew troops to defend Manchuria, bringing the fighting in south China to an end.

Although starving and low on ammunition, the Japanese soldiers fought on in the swamps and jungles of Northern Burma. This British patrol is taking no chances as it moves cautiously through a banana grove on the look out for snipers.

The monsoons turned the jungle tracks into quagmires, strangling Lieutenant-General Slim's supply lines as his men tried to follow up the Japanese retreat across Burma. These Bengali engineers are struggling to keep traffic moving along the Palel-Tamu road.

IV Corps finally crossed the Chindwin River near Sittang at the end of November and began to advance east towards the Mandalay Railway. These British troops tramp through the dust as they head into the jungle on the east bank of the river.

As IV Corps advanced east, 36th British Division advanced from Mogaung to cut the Mandalay railway at Pinwe. A light artillery battery armed with 3.7 inch howitzers exchanges fire with Japanese guns in the Burma hills.

Royal Artillery 25-pounders shell enemy positions around Pinwe as 36th Division move in to capture the town on 30 November 1944.

36th Division advanced down the Nyitkyina-Mandalay railway corridor, covering 150 miles in five months as it moved through paddy fields, elephant grass, and across flooded rivers. CSM Watkins and Private Lavell of the South Wales Borderers make their way past a pagoda in Bahe as they advance towards Mandalay.

Vice-Admiral Lord Louis Mountbatten, Supreme Allied Commander of South East Asia, keeps the front line soldiers up to date with news of successes across Northern Burma.

Thick jungle and fanatical resistance by the Japanese hampered the American advance along the Lei-Kang Road. Medics run forward to rescue a wounded man from the thick undergrowth while the rest of the platoon hugs the ground. (111-SC-200025)

G Is of the 475th Regiment sweat in the heat of the sun as they march across towards their objective on the Burma Road. (111-SC-200026)

A K-9 dog handler leads a squad across a rickety bamboo bridge during the attack on the village of Namhkam. (111-SC-200142)

The First Chinese Army from Burma met 53rd Army troops advancing from China at Muse village on 22 January. Before heading into the mountains to hunt down the Japanese, these troops share Wingate ration packs.
(111-SC-200200)

Two Chinese soldiers compare equipment as the two Armies meet at Muse. The soldier on the left wears the standard Chinese uniform while his comrade is wearing American equipment.
(111-SC-200325)

Meanwhile, Fourteenth Army continued to push along the Chindwin River and was within sixty miles of Mandalay by the end of January 1945. Indian troops advance through flames and smoke to clear the village of Mudalih.

Britsh armour was deployed in strength for the first time on Christmas Day, pushing thirty miles towards Pyingyaing in two days. This column of Sherman and Lee-Grant tanks are taking advantage of the good weather to advance along a dry riverbed of the Sipadon Chaung, a monsoon river.
(111-SC-200200)

The first of many trucks snake their way across the treacherous Ledo road, the supply artery connecting Burma and India that was finally opened at the end of January. (111-SC-200037)

It took over 80,000 men two years to construct the road and malaria, mosquitoes, leeches and Japanese snipers took their toll as the work progressed at a snails pace across rivers, gorges and mountains. The drivers negotiate a tight bend and keep a watch for rock falls as they pass beneath a treacherous overhang.
(111-SC-200339)

Crowds turned out to cheer the first convoy through the streets of Kunming on 4 February 1945; it would be the first of many. Although General Stilwell had been removed at the Generalissmo's request, Chiang Kai-Shek named the road after his old advisor. (111-SC-200343)

Pontoons, rafts and motorboats ferried men and equipment across the River Irrawaddy after IV Corps crossed at Nyaungu on 14 February. The crew of a Lee-Grant wave to the cameraman as their tank drives onto the east bank of the river. (111-SC-207359)

An Indian Bren-Carrier joins the drive east across the Burma plain heading for Meiktila, the Japanese communications centre. British and Indian troops faced fanatical resistance as they closed in on the town.

Although Meiktila fell on 3 March, rearguards continued to hold out in Fort Dufferin for another eighteen days as tanks, artillery and bombers pounded the ancient fortifications. These Lee tanks are moving towards the walls of the fort as soldiers of the 19th Indian Division move in for the final assault.

On 13 March 26th Indian Division landed on Ramree Island on the west coast of Burma to seize airfields and form a staging area for XV Corps amphibious attack on Rangoon. These landing craft are just returning from the beachhead to collect another load of troops from the British destroyers waiting offshore. (111-SC-207533)

A Bren-Carrier crashes through the jungle during the advance along the Irrawaddy Basin road as Fourteenth Army closed in on Mandalay.

XV Corps launched Operation DRACULA on 2 May, a combined amphibious and airborne attack, against Rangoon but the assault waves of 26th Indian Division discovered that the Japanese had already withdrawn from the city. Ghurkas wade across the muddy banks of the Rangoon River to their assembly point. (111-SC-207555)

Indian troops pour ashore to join the final attack across the Sittang River where the Japanese had chosen to make their final stand along the Thailand border. (111-SC-207655)

By the end of July, Japanese resistance in Burma had ended. Thousands of British, American, Indian and Chinese troops had been killed, wounded or succumbed to disease during the bitter campaign and the exhaustion on the faces of these Ghurkas is plain to see.

7th Australian Division landed on the coast of Borneo at Balikpapan on 1 July 1945 to capture one of the main sources of Japanese fuel oil. Aussies of 18th Brigade wade ashore on Red Beach as warships pound Japanese positions covering the beach. (111-SC-210699)

With the beach secure, larger landing craft can start to land reinforcements and tanks to support the push inland. (111-SC-210252)

Infantry pick their way through shattered tree stumps as they approach the Japanese positions on the summit of Hill 87 overlooking the beach. The Allied Air Forces dropped 3,000 tonnes of bombs and US Seventh Fleet fired 38,000 shells against the Balikpapan defences before the Australians landed. (111-SC-210249)

A forward observer team directs mortar and artillery fire onto the enemy positions on Hill 87, only 750 metres from the beach. (111-SC-210250)

A Howitzer of the 2nd/4th Australian Field Regiment pounds the Japanese strongpoints with high explosives. (111-SC-210442)

A Vickers Machine Gun team gives covering fire for the infantry of 18th Australian Infantry Brigade. (111-SC-210438)

Infantry take cover as Matilda tanks advance through the burning storage tanks of the Royal Shell Oil Company installation. (111-SC-210702)

The commander of a Matilda braces himself as his tank crashes through a barricade. Within days over half of the 4,000 strong garrison had been killed; the remainder fled into the hills to wait for the end of the war. (111-SC-210704)

On 12 September a convoy of ships carried troops to Singapore to accept the surrender of the garrison. Soldiers watch as British ships sail into the habour for the first time in three and a half years. (111-SC-341690)

Occupation troops disembark at Singapore docks, scene of the humiliating surrender of British troops in February 1942. Hours later Lord Louis Mountbatten would accept the surrender of the Japanese forces in Malaya bringing the fighting in South East Asia to an end. (111-SC-341689)

Chapter Two

S-Day on Luzon
and the drive to Manila

Since General Douglas MacArthur had been forced to evacuate the Philippine Islands in the spring of 1942, he had been determined to return, not only to free the local population from the oppressive Japanese régime, but as the first stage on the road to his final objective, the defeat of Japan.

Success at sea in 1944 had paved the way for MacArthur's plans and after the Japanese Navy had been crippled in the battle for the Philippine Sea in June, it was virtually destroyed in the battle for Leyte Gulf four months later. It meant that the Americans could deploy their battle fleets and invasion flotillas wherever they wanted and the capture of Leyte Island in December 1944 was the first small step on the road to conquering the Philippines. Next came Mindoro, a small outlying island, and the under strength Japanese garrison could do little to stop the American landings. Within two weeks of landing, two airstrips were operational and for the first time US fighters could counter Japanese air power and respond to the rising threat from suicidal kamikaze pilots.

The main centre of Japanese resistance in the Philippines was on Luzon Island, the largest in the group, and General Yamashita had 260,000 men deployed in three separate areas ready to meet MacArthur's invasion. Shobu Group had spent weeks preparing fortifications across the hills in the north of the island while Shimbu Group dug in across the mountains east of Manila, protecting the reservoirs supplying Manila with fresh water. Kembu Group, held Bataan Peninsula and Corregidor Island covering the approaches to the capital.

On 9 January, S-Day, I Corps and XIV Corps made an unopposed landing in Lingayen Gulf and began to move inland. Over the days that followed Sixth Army brought 175,000 men ashore on a twenty-mile wide beachhead and while I Corps protected the flanks, XIV Corps prepared to advance across the island to attack the capital. Meanwhile, a second landing, codenamed MIKE VI, had been made on the southern end of the island, opening a second front.

The drive to Manila began on 18 January and five days later, General Griswold's leading column ran into Kembu Group on Clark Field on the outskirts of the city. MacArthur was unhappy with the speed of the advance and while he urged his

The landings on Mindoro were unopposed and, by the end of the first day, Army engineers had started to build the first airstrip on the island. Two were completed in thirteen days. The new airbase allowed American aircraft to protect future invasion fleets from kamikaze attacks. (111-SC-2000009)

subordinates to push on, 1st Cavalry Division sent a flying column racing ahead while the rest of Griswold's divisions struggled to make progress.

The Cavalry entered Manila on 3 February and while the rest of XIV Corps moved in to tighten the noose around the capital, Japanese troops abandoned the suburbs and pulled back across the Pasig River, finding refuge in the old town.

The battle quickly degenerated into house-to-house fighting but with help from their Philippino allies, Griswold's divisions crossed the river over the days that followed. Strongholds were cleared one by one and the two main centres of resistance on Provisor Island and Nicols Field had fallen by 11 February. It was only a matter of time before the city was taken, and the fall of the main Finance Building on 4 March heralded the end. It would be some time before the last Japanese soldier was cleared from Manila but MacArthur had returned.

Over 175,000 assembled for the landings on Luzon requiring a huge flotilla of landing craft and amphibious vehicles of all shapes and sizes. Troops load a landing craft with supplies in the foreground while amphibious Alligators line up along the beach ready to load into a waiting LSM. (111-SC-200008)

As his landing craft sails towards Luzon, Private Ernest Gosbee takes time to read the latest Army handbook, *How the Japanese Army Fights*. (111-SC-282230)

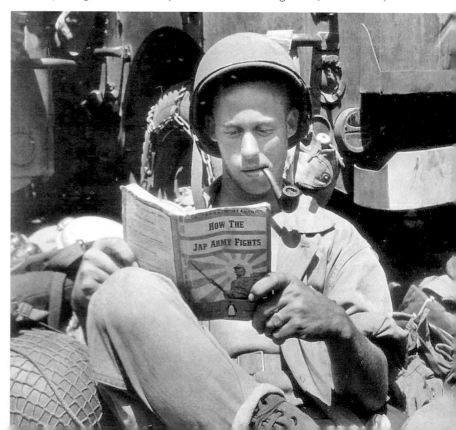

The weather on the morning of 9 January, S-Day, was ideal for Sixth Army's landing; gentle waves and a light overcast sky gave GIs a smooth ride onto the beach. The naval bombardment began at 07:00 and an hour later the first troops hit the shore. (111-SC-265298)

LST 22 unloads its cargo of amphibious vehicles into the sea off the coast of Lingayen Gulf. These Alligators and Buffaloes carried the first wave of 43rd Division's troops ashore. (111-SC-200500)

General Yamashita had chosen to concentrate his troops inland and resistance was light at most points. These men of 43rd Division have come under fire 300 yards from the shoreline on White Beach, and have dismounted from their Alligator to return fire. (111-SC-2000019)

31

Before long troops were pushing inland all along Sixth Army's front and 43rd Division, living up to its nickname, the Winged Victory Division, advanced towards the town of San Fabian. (111-SC-200141)

Sixth Army soldiers had to fight their way through tangled undergrowth and cross a network of watercourses beyond the beach. These men are holding their weapons high as they wade across a stream. (111-SC-200017)

Japanese engineers destroyed the Calmay Bridge ahead of the 37th Buckeye Division and the GIs of 148th Regiment had to negotiate a narrow gangplank to cross the river. (111-SC-200010)

General Oscar Griswold was anxious to establish a deep beachhead as soon as possible so that Japanese artillery could not target the huge numbers of landing craft gathered along the shoreline. A Sherman tank, still sporting the air intakes needed to negotiate shallow water, passes the Municipal Hall in Lingayen town. (111-SC-2000005)

The main drive was going to be directed towards the island's capital, Manila, but to begin with General Kruger made sure his flanks were secure. Before long, heavy artillery was ashore and able to support the ground troops as they sealed off the roads into the mountains to the north. The crew of this 155mm gun are kept busy shelling Japanese positions near Urdaneta. (111-SC-200765)

A squad had just come under fire in thick undergrowth and this heavy machine gun are trying to locate the Japanese position so they can give covering fire.

25th Division drove across the Luzon Central Plain, meeting the enemy at Binalonan on 17 January. Sergeant Bill Soklecki has just located the entrance of an underground bunker and is taking no chances, giving it the full attention of his flamethrower. (111-SC-200767)

25th Division pushed on through the rice paddies into Umingan, Lupao, and San Jose where supporting tanks destroyed a large part of the Japanese armour stationed on Luzon. The crew of Classy Peg manage to squeeze their Sherman past the burning wreck of a Japanese medium tank in the village of Linganmansan. (111-SC-200644)

While engineers use a mixture of dynamite and petrol to blow the roof off a bunker, the infantry stand by ready to shoot any Japanese forced out by the flames. (111-SC-200763)

General MacArthur became increasingly frustrated by the slow and deliberate build-up beyond the beachhead and continually pressed General Kruger to drive on Manila. This was one of the first pictures taken of MacArthur after he had been awarded his fifth star; they are proudly displayed on his collar. (111-SC-200507)

XIV Corps eventually moved south towards the city on 18 January but MacArther was still unhappy with the rate of progress. These men of the 40th Grizzly Division are finding it tough going as they head off towards their objective. (111-SC-265273)

Close support between the infantry and tanks was needed in the jungle, but progress was slow. Infantry look out for snipers in the undergrowth as the tanks crawl forward towards the Japanese stronghold of Damortis. (111-SC-200590)

XIV Corps's advance for Manila began on 18 January and the crew of this LVT are ready to take a bite at the Japanese as they head for Clark Field. (111-SC-200060)

A second amphibious, Operation MIKE VI, was made to the southwest of Manila on 15 January; the race to reach the city first was on. Japanese soldiers tried to burn down the bridge over Matain River but tanks continued to roll across while GIs fought the fires. (111-SC-200409)

On 31 January, X-Ray Day, two regiments of the 11th Airborne Division were dropped south of Manila and captured a nearby bridge before the Japanese could demolish it. The division's third regiment followed, landing on Taygaytay Ridge, and before long the paratroopers were speeding north toward the capital. (111-SC-263736)

As American troops were converging on Manila from three directions, the local population did what they could to help their liberators. General Robert Eichelberger, Eight Army's commander, has stopped fifteen miles from the city to talk to Philippino guerrillas. (111-SC-263724)

General MacArthur told Major-General Verne Mudge to 'go to Manila, go around the Nips, bounce off the Nips, but go to Manila' and after racing at speeds of up to fifty miles an hour, 1st Cavalry Division's Flying Column won the race, reaching the outskirts of the capital on 3 February. The locals have turned out in force to greet the Americans. (111-SC-264209)

Although the shantytowns on Manila's outskirts were cleared quickly, Rear Admiral Iwabachi Sanji was determined to hold the centre of the city. Huge clouds of smoke rise from the docks and every bridge leading into the walled city beyond the Pansig River has been destroyed; the battle of the city was about to begin. (111-SC-200052)

After the elation of the drive into the outskirts of Manila, the battle for the city quickly degenerated into a series of bitter street battles as the Japanese made their last stand. There is an enemy strongpoint at the end of this street and while GIs shelter in doorways to keep a watch for snipers, the crew of a 37mm gun wheel their weapon into position. (111-SC-200312)

Japanese engineers demolished military installations and important buildings as they withdrew towards the Parsig River in front of 37th Division. These men have located a machine gun post firing from this upper storey window and are preparing to storm the building. (111-SC-200553)

One group of Japanese made a last stand on Provisor Island, a small industrial zone on the Pansig River. This .05 machine-gun crew have set their weapon up on the third floor of the Manila National Bank so they can fire at targets across the river. (111-SC-263664)

General MacArthur placed strict limitations on artillery and air support to try and reduce civilian casualties but there was still widespread devastation across the city. A battery from 61st Field Artillery Battalion fires their 105mm Howitzers at targets in the walled city. (111-SC-265337)

Nuns and soldiers work together to evacuate injured civilians from a damaged building in the Intramuras Quarter of the city. (111-SC-263686)

The Tetran Building on the banks of the Pansig River was one centre of resistance; smoke and dust erupt as a 155mm shell slams into the walls. (111-SC-263665)

37th Division found that Japanese Regular and Naval troops were preparing to make a last stand on the University Campus. Two flame-throwing tanks roll forward across a débris-strewn square to burn out a gun position that has been holding up the advance. (111-SC-263666)

A few hours after American troops entered Manila, General MacArthur announced the imminent capture of the capital; the declaration proved to be premature. The last stronghold, based around the huge Finance Building in the walled city did not fall until 4 March. Private Okonski snipes at Japanese positions covering the Jones Bridge, one of the many crossings over the Pansig that had been demolished by Japanese engineers. (111-SC-263667)

The 16,000 strong Manila Naval Defence Force and the three Regular Battalions, sent to bolster the sailors, were virtually wiped out during the month-long battle for the city. American casualties were also high and these two GIs were pictured helping their wounded buddy to the aid station during the final days.
(111-SC-265368)

Chapter Three

The Campaigns against Simbu Group and Shobu Group

As XIV Corps raced towards Manila, two divisions from XI Corps carried out an unopposed landing on Bataan Peninsula, the neck of land forming the western side of Manila Bay. General Charles Hall's men advanced quickly across the peninsula, finding Philippino guerrillas holding San Marcelino airstrip, and had reached the opposite coast in less than twenty-four hours. Turning south, XI Corps lined up in front of the Zambales Mountains where Colonel Nagayoshi and 4,000 soldiers were holding prepared defences either side of Zig-Zig Pass. Attacks on the flanks of the Japanese line broke through on 8 February and, as the few survivors fled into the jungle, General Hall announced that the peninsula was clear.

On 16 February, Sixth Army launched a combined air and sea attack on Corregidor Island, a small outcrop guarding the entrance to the harbour. As 503rd Parachute Regiment landed on Topside Hill, the highest point on the island, a battalion of infantry landed on the shore, surprising the garrison. The fortress was taken after a week of heavy fighting.

As the fighting in Manila came to a close, XIV Corps crossed Marikina Valley on 20 February and probed the hills to the east. The advance came to a standstill on Mount Pacawagan and Mount Mataba, an area honeycombed with bunkers and tunnels. For two weeks XIV Corps struggled to climb the hills but on 12 March General Yokoyama handed General Griswold the advantage by launching a disastrous counterattack. Shimbu Group fled into the hills where it continued to fight for another two months; Ipo Dam was finally taken on 17 May, soon followed by Wawa Dam. The survivors refused to surrender and hundreds held out in the Sierra Madre Mountains in eastern Luzon until the end of the war.

Shimbu Group's positions on the Bicol Peninsula suffered a similar fate. XIV Corps attacked the line between Laguna Bay and Batangas Bay on 19 March and had reached the vital road junction at Santo Tomas by the end of the month. On 1 April troops landed on the tip of the peninsula behind the Japanese lines and before long Shimbu Group had been surrounded. Organised resistance came to an end on 19 April.

In the north, I Corps had been probing Shobu Group's positions covering Bambang since the end of February but 33rd Division had failed to make any

On 29 January 38th Division landed unopposed on the Bataan Peninsula and lived up to its nickname as it moved quickly inland like a Cyclone to engage the Nagayoshi Detachment. (111-SC-341682)

headway along Route 11. However, reconnaissance troops had pushed north along the unguarded coast, opening a new road into Shobu Group's stronghold along Route 9. With the help of 37th Division, guerrillas and airstrikes, the Japanese forces were pushed back across the Irisan River, and days later Baguio fell. It marked the beginning of the end for Shobu Group. Sixth Army pushed deeper into the hills forcing General Yamashita's men to scatter into the Asin Valley area of northern Luzon. Although thousands died of starvation and disease, the survivors refused to surrender and over 50,000 eventually emerged from the jungle at the end of the war.

The March of Death in reverse. After the Japanese occupied Luzon in 1942, American Prisoners of War had been forced to march under brutal conditions to their prison camps. These GIs of 149th Regiment keep a sharp lookout for Japanese snipers as they take their first steps along the trail. (111-SC-263694)

The men who fought to defend Luzon between December 1941 and April 1942 called themselves the *Battling Bastards of Bataan* but their fight was in vain and after their surrender the men of the Philippine Division faced three years of captivity under their brutal guards. 38th Division retraced the route in the spring of 1945 and Major-General Frederick Irving's men coined a new nickname, the *Avengers of Bataan*. (111-SC-264263)

The Angels have landed. 503rd Parachute Regiment dropped onto Topside Hill, the highest point of Corregidor Island on 16 February prior to the sea borne landing; hundreds of parachutes litter the rugged slopes of the tiny island. (111-SC-200787)

There was nowhere to hide on B Field and the paratroopers untangle themselves before the inevitable Japanese counter-attack begins. Private Lloyd McCarter was awarded the Medal of Honour for charging a key enemy position and knocking out a machine gun nest with hand grenades. (111-SC-201041)

Paratrooper Thomas Barnes counts himself lucky after the landing on Corrigedor Island. A sniper's bullet pierced his helmet moments after hitting the ground. (111-SC-201308)

As soon as the paratroopers had cleared the high ground a battalion of the 34th Infantry from the 24th Victory Division stormed ashore onto the only suitable beach on the island.
(111-SC-200884)

The Japanese garrison held out for ten days under a hot sun on the well-defended Rock. Paratroopers detonate explosives at the mouth of a bunker while the crew of a machine gun waits to see if any enemy soldiers emerge after the dust has cleared.
(111-SC-201037)

Sixth Army began its attack on Shimbu Group on 20 February and 6th Division's first objective was to clear Mount Pacawagan and Mount Mataba. This GI surveys the mountainous country he will have to fight over as the division lives up to its nickname, the Sight-Seeing Sixth.

1st Cavalry Division crossed the Marikina Valley with ease, finding the Japanese holding the hills beyond. San Tomas was attacked next and Philippino guerrillas worked alongside 7th and 8th Cavalry Brigade to clear the town. (111-SC-264116)

A foothold was seized on Mount Pacawagan as early as 4 March and four days later the GIs made headway up the slopes of Mount Mataba but savage fighting would continue for another week. After each small advance flamethrower teams followed up to make sure every bunker and dugout was clear. (111-SC-264916)

Total cooperation between all arms was needed before a successful attack could be launched. A P-38 swoops in low overhead to drop two 300lb bombs while the GI sitting on the Sherman uses the tank's radio to call in close artillery support on the Japanese positions covering the road. (111-SC-264187)

After the air and artillery strikes have finished, the infantry fix bayonets and move in using smoke grenades to cover their advance through the jungle. (111-SC-200401)

38th Cyclone Division joined Sixth Army and pushed back General Shizuo's southern flank, leading to a general withdrawal and the end of Shimbu Group. Ipo Dam was captured on 17 May, restoring Manila's water supply and these prepare to give covering fire as a patrol move in on the division's next objective, Wawa Dam. (111-SC-209208)

General Shizuo launched a counter-attack on 12 April with disastrous results; it failed to drive 6th Division off the hills and only served to hasten Shimbu Group's demise. GIs advance across a shell torn summit, driving the survivors deeper into the Sierra Madre Mountains. (111-SC-264215)

Mopping up operations continued until the end of the war and hundreds of Japanese soldiers died from disease and hunger in the Sierra Madre Mountains in eastern Luzon. Rocks, earth and debris fly into the air as another bunker is blown sky high by a satchel charge. (111-SC-209028)

Major-General Sumi, Shimbu Group's Chief of Staff, emerges from the jungle on 26 August to begin his own negotiations, two weeks after the formal surrender of the Japanese Army, . (111-SC-211255)

C Battery of 90th Field Artillery Battalion lay down a heavy barrage on the Japanese positions around Balete Pass before 25th Division launch an attack on 19 April. (111-SC-205918)

Philippinos worked together with their liberators to drive the Japanese from their country. Lieutenant Teodolso Quejano leads Corporal Maxwell Bentley's patrol through the heavily wooded hills of northern Luzon. (111-SC-263055)

Company K, 161st Regimental Combat Team blast apart Japanese bunkers in the hills above Balete Pass with a bazooka. A cloud of smoke erupts from the back of the weapon as another projectile is fired. (111-SC-264167)

Meanwhile, 33rd Red Bull Division was struggling to make progress along Highway 11 towards Bambang. This machine gun team is giving covering fire as 130th Regiment's 1st Battalion tries to cross the Bauang River Bridge. (111-SC-345118)

Sergeant Wilburn Kirksley keeps a sharp lookout during 161st Regiment's advance over the hills surrounding Balete Pass. His patrol had spotted a Japanese patrol only a few moments before and killed one; another escaped but the third was cornered behind a rock and committed suicide rather than surrender. (111-SC-206252)

After making little progress along Highway 11, 33rd Division changed tack and pushed a task force along Route 9 heading for Baguio. This patrol of 130th Regiment found little to stop them as they advanced towards General Yamashita's headquarters. Some men have hitched a lift on the self-propelled 105mm gun carriage. (111-SC-206277)

There was nothing to stop 33rd Division once the Irisan River had been crossed. Company D of 129th Regiment hitch a ride into Baguio on Shermans of the 775th Tank Battalion. (111-SC-263053)

Signal Corps cameramen were sometimes forced to fight alongside the GIs as they tried to photograph or film the action. Technician Gae Faillace was weighed down with cameras and equipment when a Japanese soldier attacked him in Baguio; Faillace won the fight. (111-SC-263038)

The fall of Baguio signalled the beginning of the end for the Shobu group, however, thousands of Japanese soldiers continued to fight on in the hills surrounding the Cagayan Valley. 251st Field Artillery Battalion supports an attack by 145th Regiment as it closes in on the village of Crodon along Highway 5. (111-SC-209764)

Lieutenant Lloyd Smith's team keep their mortar busy during the attack on Crodon. (111-SC-209766)

37th Division joined the fight and with the help of Filipino guerrillas began to move in on Japanese strongholds. 775th Tank Battalion provides support as the division attacks Lantap. (111-SC-209769)

Japanese troops relied on suicidal tactics to destroy tanks, running out of the undergrowth in the hope of throwing a satchel charge into one of the hatches. The tank crews relied on the infantry to keep them at bay. This Sherman blasts a way forward along Highway 4 during 37th Division's advance on Lantap. (111-SC-209762)

Private Robert Miles was confronted by this Japanese soldier as he ran down Highway 5. Miles fired first and then dropped to the ground to engage snipers in the undergrowth ahead. (111-SC-209767)

This Japanese supply column was caught in the open by American planes as it tried to escape from Lantap; GIs survey the devastation as they take a break. (111-SC-209760)

As there were no Japanese planes over Luzon, this self-propelled anti-aircraft weapon of 209th AAA Battalion is put to good use in a ground fighting role. The quad barrelled .30 machine guns spray the undergrowth before the tanks advance towards Kiangan. (111-SC-211290)

General Tomoyuki Yamashita, the Tiger of Malaya, remained defiant to the end. He eventually emerged from his jungle hiding place to meet Major-General Robert Beightler, commander of the 37th Division, after the signing of the formal surrender in Japan. (111-SC-263528)

Japanese soldiers continued to hold out in the Asin Valley area of Sierra Madre until the end of the war. General Yamashita and over 50,000 eventually surrendered after the close of hostilities on 15 August; thousands more had perished as disease and starvation took their toll. Sergeant Edgar Fultz searches his prisoner during 32nd Division's drive across the Cagayan valley. (111-SC-209593)

Chapter Four

Clearing the
Southern Philippines

As the battle for Luzon progressed, Eighth Army planned a new campaign to clear the islands of the Southern Philippines and although General MacArthur never received specific orders to start the operation, he believed that the islands would serve as an additional staging area for the final assault on Japan; Operations VICTOR I to VICTOR V would also free the islanders from the Japanese regime.

On 28 February 41st Division made the first amphibious landing on Palawan and after a week of bitter fighting, the Japanese garrison withdrew into the hills; it would take two more months to clear the island. The rest of 41st Division landed on Zamboanga Peninsula on 10 March and after taking the capital, drove the Japanese force into the hills where fighting continued until June. The division's final operation was to clear the Sulu Archipelago, a string of tiny islands. Finding the main force concentrated on Jolo; it took two weeks to clear the 4,000 strong garrison from the slopes of Mount Daho in the centre of the island.

Philippino guerrillas controlled the countryside on Panay, Negros, Cebu, and Bohol, helping both 40th Division and the Americal Division in their conquest of the group of islands. Operation VICTOR I opened on 18 March with a landing on Panay and a week later Operation VICTOR II began on Cebu Island. Two landings on Negros brought the operations to an end and by the beginning of June organised resistance had come to an end; hundreds of Japanese would continue to hold out in the mountains until the end of the war.

The final objective in Eighth Army's campaign was Mindanao, the second largest island in the Philippines and 24th Division opened the campaign with an unopposed landing on the west coast on 17 April. Moving quickly along Highway 1, the Americans bypassed the main Japanese defences and had seized the capital, Davao City before General Morozumi realised that the landing had not been a feint; the division had moved over one hundred miles through inhospitable terrain in two weeks. Meanwhile, gunboats had sailed up the Mindanao River, paving the way for 31st Division's landing on 22 April but a combination of poor weather and terrain made it impossible to advance quickly north towards Kibawe. Jungle rain forest and

After fighting their way across the Pacific, the men of the 41st Division began to call themselves the Jungleers. The invasion of the Zamoanga Peninsula on 10 March, part of Operation VICTOR IV, was unopposed; it was the lull before the storm. (111-SC-263704)

torrential rain allowed the Japanese to conduct a fighting withdrawal along the Sayre Highway but the outcome was inevitable. Further landings along the coast helped to speed up the American advance and by the end of June the two Japanese divisions on the island had ceased to exist, bringing organised resistance in the Southern Philippines to an end.

GIs of 163rd Regiment hug the ground as mortars supporting 54th Independent Mixed Brigade zero in on their positions. (111-SC-263705)

Tanks were able to operate in the open area along the coast and before long the Japanese withdrew from the city of Zamboanga and headed for the hills. This Sherman, called Iron Horse by its crew, moves forward while enemy mortars fire from hidden positions. (111-SC-263707)

A plentiful supply of ammunition keeps this platoon of 81mm mortars busy as it supports the Jungleers attack on the hills overlooking the city. Organised resistance came to an end at the end of March but hundreds of Japanese soldiers withdrew into the jungle rather than surrender. (111-SC-264205)

The 3,900 strong garrison on the Sulu Archipelago chose to make their stand on Mount Daho in the centre of the island. The mountain was taken on 22 April but Japanese troops continued to harass 163rd Regiment for another two months. These men are using a flamethrower to make sure that a bunker is clear before moving on. (111-SC-207519)

A moment's respite for Private Ernest Carahajal during the savage fighting for Mount Daho; a copy of the latest issue of 41st Division's newspaper, *Front Lines*, has just arrived. Many divisions produced newsletters full of cartoons, jokes and reports on the progress of the war around the world. (111-SC-262936)

A rare sight; this GI smiles for the camera as he leads a Japanese Marine into captivity. Many Japanese soldiers chose to fight to the death or commit suicide; others withdrew into the hills and refused to surrender, and hundreds died of starvation and disease. (111-SC-262979)

23,000 Philippino guerrillas had forced the Japanese into their fortifications around the town of Iloilo on the island of Panay. Colonel Peralta's men treated 185th Regiment to a parade shortly after they landed. (111-SC-263778)

Privates Paul Wellvang and Harold Smith prepare to give covering fire for 1st Battalion during 185th Regiment's attack on Iloilo. The cameraman, Lieutenant Robert Fields was killed shortly after taking this photograph. (111-SC-263766)

Infantry take cover while Sherman tanks rumble forward, firing point blank into enemy positions near Maloy. With no armour of their own, the Japanese had no option but to withdraw into the mountains. (111-SC-263761)

After the fall of Iloilo a single battalion of 185th Regiment stayed behind on Pannay to help the guerrillas round up the remaining Japanese troops on the island. Over 1,500 held out until the end of the war. These GIs are trying to track down a sniper in the thick undergrowth, typical of the mountain jungles on the island. (111-SC-263776)

General Eichelberger had split the island of Negros into two sectors, with the central highlands as a dividing line. 40th Division made the first landing on the northwest coast as part of Operation VICTOR I on 29 March and quickly pushed inland; this company is moving into the jungle to outflank Japanese positions covering Bacolod airfield. (111-SC-264217)

The rest of 40th Division opened Operation VICTOR II on 26 March with a landing on Cebu Island. Men of 3rd Battalion, on 132nd Regiment's front, come under fire as they move up the beach. Minefields in the undergrowth beyond the shoreline destroyed ten of the first fifteen LVTs ashore. (111-SC-204236)

After securing Cebu City, 182nd Infantry attacked two strongly defended hills to the north but Japanese engineers detonated an ammunition dump as Company A advanced over their positions, killing and wounding GIs in the explosion. Tracer bullets light up the night sky in the hills around Cebu in the hope of preventing Japanese counter-attacks. (111-SC-205889)

A second landing on the southeast coast of Negros followed the capture of Cebu at the culmination of Operation VICTOR II. 164th Regiment moved quickly along the coast and made contact with 40th Division's Reconnaissance Troop before moving into the hills. Although over four thousand Japanese troops were killed, another ten thousand were determined to hold out in the hills. Hundreds had died of starvation and disease by the time the war ended. (111-SC-206924)

Operation VICTOR V, the invasion of Mindanao, began on 17 April and after landing on the undefended west coast, 24th Victory Division began to drive east towards Davao along Highway 1. This advance patrol of 19th Regiment scouts ahead of the main body along the nipa tree lined Highway 1. (111-SC-207505)

After gunboats of the 3rd Engineer Special Brigade had cleared the Mindanao River on 21 April, the waterway became 24th Division's main supply line across the island. GIs of 34th Regiment enjoy the ride inland as they are transported to Kabacan. (111-SC-207688)

31st Dixie Division came ashore on 22 April and advanced north up the Sayre Highway heading towards Macajalar Bay. Japanese engineers destroyed the Mutian Bridge as they withdrew, and these men are forced to use a lifeline to climb down the steep sided ravine so they can cross the river. (111-SC-270988)

24th Division's rapid advance to Davao City cut General Morozumi's forces in two, allowing X Corps to deal with each group in turn. Thousands of locusts rise into the air as a patrol advances through the jungle towards Digos on the east coast of the island. (111-SC-262948)

Private George Updike holds a battle-scarred Rising Sun flag aloft after the assault on Davao: it had been wrapped around the waist of a dead Japanese soldier. After the city was taken on 3 May there was no doubt about the outcome of the campaign, however, Morozumi's men withdrew into hills and jungles to fight until the end of the war. (111-SC-262945

Chapter Five

D-Day on Iwo Jima and the Battle for Mount Suribachi

Iwo Jima, a small spit of volcanic rock halfway between Saipan and Tokyo, was Japan's main radar station for warning against long range bombing raids on the homeland. Admiral Chester Nimitz, the Pacific Ocean's commander, intended to take the island to increase the effectiveness of the American bombing campaign, Sulphur Island would also be serve as an ideal advanced airbase. Operation DETACHMENT was an important stepping-stone on the road to Japan, for the first time American troops would be fighting inside Japan's inner defence line.

D-Day was set for 19 February and while Fifth Fleet's range of battleships, cruisers and destroyers pounded targets along the shore, hundreds of landing craft and amphibious vehicles, V Amphibious Corps sailed towards the thin strip of black sand on the southeast coast of the island. Heavy fire met the landing force as it approached the shoreline, but as wave after wave of Marines hit the beaches, men crawled and ran forward towards their objectives.

On 5th Division's front, 28th Marines advanced inland from Green Beach across the foot of Mount Suribachi, the volcanic outcrop at the south end of the island, while 25th Marines moved off Red Beach towards Airstrip One. Meanwhile, 4th Division met the Japanese headlong on the right flank, and as the 23rd Marines fought their way off Yellow Beach, 25th Marines were pinned down on Blue Beach.

As men, tanks and guns clogged up the shoreline, General Kuribayashi's gunners unmasked their artillery and started to cause mayhem on the crowded beach. For a time it seemed as though the Marines would be thrown back into the sea but as the survivors took stock of the situation, naval and air support helped them inch forward. By noon 28th Marines had reached the west coast of the island and the rest of the line was moving forward across the airfield. By nightfall, General Schmidt had over 30,000 men ashore, and although the two assault divisions had suffered over 2,400 casualties, both were moving forward towards their objectives; the Marines were here to stay.

By the morning of the second day, five infantry regiments faced General Kuribayashi's positions on the high ground to the north while 28th Marines had turned south to attack Mount Suribachi. The heavy bombardment failed to dislodge

Marines of LT3, Combat Team 26, cross the forward well deck of their landing craft to their disembarkation stations. (127-GW-112470)

the Japanese from their bunkers and caves and anti-tank guns took their toll as 5th Tank Battalion's Shermans advanced but the Marines advanced two hundred metres, losing a man for each metre. The rest of General Schmidt's men continued to advance across the centre of the island, and as 5th Division cleared Airstrip One, 4th Division edged forward onto the high ground overlooking Rock Quarry on the right flank.

Day three was another of high casualties and small gains but, by the morning of 23 February, 28th Marines moved up the slopes of Mount Suribachi. Lieutenant Harold Schrier led a small patrol up the slopes and after a short fire-fight raised the American flag on top of the hill; the sight was a tremendous morale boost and was greeted by the sound of ship's sirens and cheers from the beach below. Sergeant Michael Strank had soon joined Schrier, bringing a larger flag to the summit and the image of the Marines lifting the Stars and Stripes on Mount Suribachi would symbolise both the battle and the US Marine Corps at war.

Troops clamber off the deck of USS Cecil and climb down the scramble nets into their landing craft; a hazardous task made difficult by the rough sea. (127-GW-110822)

All aboard. Marines of 28th Regiment try and sort themselves as they crowd into a Higgins landing craft. (127-GW-11247)

A battleship moves in to shell the area covering the landing beaches as the flotilla of landing craft and amphibious personnel carriers starts their run in; the mass of Mount Suribachi in the distance marks the southern tip of the island.

Private Kenneth Hoger has christened his flamethrower 'Miss Spitfire', one hot momma.
(127-GW-109636)

The crew of an amphibious tractor take their final instructions from one of the control boats supervising 4th Division's assembly area before heading towards the beach. (127-GW-110134)

As the naval bombardment reaches a crescendo, wave after wave of landing craft and amphibious vehicles head for the shore through the choppy waves. There was no turning back.

As surf batters the crowded Higgins boats, the Marines watch the navy shell the shore. The thought on everyone's mind is, 'Will it be enough?' (127-GW-111904)

Clear the ramps! As the coxswain slows down ready to land, bullets begin to skim across the waves. With only moments to go before the ramp drops, one marine bows his head and prays he will survive. (127-GW-110823)

Go Go Go! Bullets and shrapnel meet the Marines as they spill out onto the beach. The first wave of Combat Team 26 is already pinned down at the top of the sand bank and the second wave disembark as quickly as possible, looking to find cover on the exposed beach. (127-GW-111114)

As smoke curls around the base of Mount Surabachi the Marines of Combat Team 28 hug the volcanic sand on Green Beach as Amtracks begin to move inland. (127-GW-111690)

There is nowhere to hide as the artillery and machine guns on the mountain rake the beach with bullets and shrapnel. Bodies and debris litter the shoreline while the living try and find cover. (127-GW-111690)

Despite the heavy fire, squad leaders and platoon officers begin to gather their men together; ready to advance. This group on Green Beach are looking for the rest of their company before moving towards Suribachi, codenamed Hot Rock 10. (127-GW-110918)

25th Regiment came under intense fire as soon as it reached Blue Beach on the right flank. While 1st Battalion crawled forward, 3rd Battalion took heavy casualties trying to reach the cliffs leading to the Rock Quarry. (127-GW-110108)

While the Japanese concentrated on the Marines landing on the flanks, 27th Regiment moved quickly off Red Beach, and advanced onto the airfield reaching the south and west perimeters before noon. This Amtrac has a turret-mounted 75mm cannon, a useful weapon for knocking out bunkers. (127-GW-111687)

Casualties amongst officers were particularly heavy but the survivors managed to rally their men and lead them forwards onto the objectives. 26th Regiment landed in 5th Marine Division's sector at noon but Company I was quickly pinned down as it tried to advance. Captain Charles Easy is showing Captain Don Castle of Company H where his men are so the support weapons can give covering fire. (127-GW-111107)

In spite of the heavy fire from Mount Suribachi, 1st Battalion, 28th Marines kept moving along across the exposed narrow neck of the peninsula. Ninety minutes after landing the survivors reached the far shore, seven hundred yards away. (127-GW-109821)

After leaving the terraces of black sand covering the beach, 5th Division began moving onto Airfield 1, a shooting gallery overlooked by Mount Surabachi to the south and high ground to the north. This Marine has no other option but to grit his teeth and run for it.
(127-GW-109966)

Beyond Yellow Beach, 23rd Combat Team ran into two huge concrete pillboxes and a maze of fortified positions covering the perimeter of the airfield. Marine Private First Class Glen Murphy is taking no chances, unloading a full clip of ammunition into this bunker's aperture before moving on.
(127-GW-109920)

By noon both divisions were firmly established on the island but the Japanese still held the high ground, leaving the Marines exposed to artillery and small arms fire. Men found it impossible to dig foxholes in the fine volcanic sand and found cover where they could in shell craters; this group are regrouping ready to advance once more. (127-GW-109963)

As the leading combat teams pushed forward, the reserve combat teams started to come ashore during the afternoon. Lieutenant Michael F Keleher, a battalion surgeon, was met with the following scene as his landing craft approached Blue Beach: 'Wrecked boats, bogged-down jeeps, tractors and tanks; burning vehicles; casualties scattered all over'. (127-GW-109604)

Landing craft carrying the Marines' Shermans struggled to land and while some tanks bogged down in the soft sand, others hit mines and took hits from Japanese anti-tank guns; the lucky survivors were welcomed ashore. Air intakes designed to allow the tanks to beach in shallow water stand out at the back of this Sherman. (127-GW-109825)

As the battle raged on around the foot of Mount Surabachi and the Rock Quarry, the flow of supplies onto the beach had to be maintained. These men are struggling to pull their cart of ammunition up the beach. (127-GW-111115)

By nightfall over 30,000 Marines were ashore and V Amphibious Corps' beachhead was secure. It was time to plan for the morning and at 1st Battalion's headquarters in 26th Regiment's sector, Colonel Pollock receives his new orders; runners lie on the sand, waiting to pass on the message. (127-GW-112670)

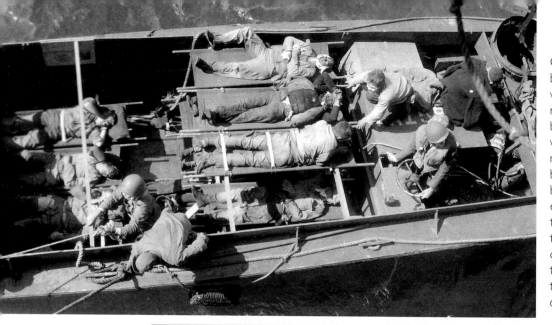

Over 2,400 men ha[d] been killed or wounded on the narrow strip of beach and there would be many more casualties before Iwo Jima had been cleared but everyone knew that the Marines were there to stay. Landin[g] craft worked aroun[d] to clock to evacuate the wounded as quickly as possible.

Others could wait; they had paid the ultimate price for fighting their way ashore. (127-GW-109624)

General Schmidt's first objective was to clear Mount Suribachi overlooking the beachhead. Japanese mortars, machine guns and anti-tank guns continued to hit the crowded shoreline as landing boats brought supplies ashore. (127-GW-110271)

The flotilla of warships kept battering the Japanese positions as reinforcements flooded ashore. The wet sand played havoc with weapons and equipment and these Marines are making sure their rifles are ready for action before moving out. (127-GW-112263)

While five Regiments swung into line to face the high ground to the north, 28th Marines prepared for the toughest task of all, the capture of Mount Suribachi. As USMC fighters dive bomb Hotrocks, 105mm howitzers of the 13th Marines join in the bombardment. They would hardly touch the concrete pillboxes and tunnels that riddled the hill. (127-GW-110141)

While the rest of 4th Division cleared the airstrip, 24th Marines fought their way onto the high ground above the Rock Quarry, losing over one hundred men; many of them from friendly fire. There are anxious faces all along the front as zero hour approaches.
(127-GW-111245)

Flamethrowers were particularly useful for clearing bunkers and the Japanese snipers kept a special lookout for Marines carrying the loathsome weapons. The distinctive shape of the fuel pack and nozzle pick this man out as he runs forward.
(127-GW-111006)

With bayonet fixed, a Marine risks sniper fire to call out mortar hits on his platoon in the hope of locating the Japanese position for the artillery. 28th Marines advanced two hundred metres on 20 February, losing a man every metre of the way. (127-GW-109954)

Hidden anti-tank guns at the base of Mount Suribachi took their toll on 5th Tank Battalion's Shermans and artillery targeted the machines each time the crews withdrew to refuel and rearm. A Sherman, nicknamed Bed Bug, crawls forward as Marines wait for the order to advance. (127-GW-109666)

Over sixty camouflage pillboxes protected the approaches to Mount Suribachi; another fifty had been dug into the slopes of the hill and they were all linked by tunnels and caves. These Marines are trying to coax a wounded soldier out of his dugout.
(127-GW-111384)

As wind and rain lashed the island, 28th Marines renewed its attack on the hill and although 1st Battalion was able to reach the southern shoulder, the rest of the Regiment failed to advance. This young Marine watches intently for signs of movement as he moves in on a Japanese bunker.
(127-GW-112862)

By 22 February progress was being made on all fronts and while 28th Marines prepared to make the final assault on Mount Suribachi, all five Regiment's in the north had footholds on the high ground. Reinforcements move across the bare landscape towards the frontline. (127-GW-109975)

Sergeant Michael Strank found a larger flag onboard LST 779 and led a second patrol to the summit. Now everyone could see Stars and Stripes flying proudly on top of the mountain. These artillery observers are using a high-powered telescope to spot enemy positions. (127-GW-113721)

Early on 23 February Captain Dave Severance ordered Lieutenant Harold Schrier to take his platoon and try to plant an American flag on the top of the mountain. After a few firefights the small group made it to the summit and with the help of an old piece of pipe raised the Stars and Stripes. All eyes turned to the top of Hotrocks as ships sounded their horns and men cheered; it was the turning point of the battle. (127-GW-112449)

Although the summit of Mount Suribachi had been taken, hundreds of Japanese soldiers continued to hold the bunkers and caves covering the slopes. Explosives send debris and dust flying into the air as another bunker disintegrates. (127-GW-112714)

Although it took several more days to clear the mountain, its loss was a severe blow to General Kuribayashi, it meant that the Marines could turn all their attentions north. Engineers burn out another dugout while landing craft deliver their load onto the beaches in the background.

Snipers frequently tried to reoccupy bunkers after they had been captured. Marine engineers were left with no choice; every one of them had to be destroyed.
(127-GW-109608)

Over 2,000 Japanese soldiers and sailors were killed or captured on Mount Suribachi: 28th Marines suffered 900 casualties taking the hill. This Japanese soldier fought to the last, firing his Nambu 6.5mm automatic rifle at the advancing Marines.
(127-GW-111007)

With the beachhead secure, it was time to prepare for the next stage of the battle. 4th Division's commander, Major Generals Clifton Cates came ashore on 23 February to plan his attack on the area known as The Meatgrinder. (127-GW-142116)

Chapter Six

Fighting to the Bitter End on Iwo Jima

The summit of Mount Suribachi was captured on 23 February and while fighting continued in the bunkers and tunnels underneath the hill for several days, General Schmidt turned his attention to the northern end of the island. All three divisions of V Amphibious Corps began to advance across Airstrip Two on D+5 towards the Japanese held high ground. 4th Marine Division became heavily engaged in an area known as the Meatgrinder on the west coast and on features codenamed Hill 382, the Amphitheatre and the Turkey Knob the Marines found that *'the Japs were not on Iwo Jima, they were in Iwo Jima'*. 5th Marine Division was heavily engaged on Nishi Ridge and the Gorge on the east coast but 3rd Marine Division made the main attack across Airstrip Two in the centre of the island. Marines mounted on Sherman tanks charged across the airfield only to find the Japanese dug in on two hills known as Peter and 199-Oboe at the far side. It would take three days to take them.

The hills were cleared one by one as flamethrower tanks and engineers burnt and blew the bunkers and caves apart, but Schmidt's casualties mounted in what was quickly degenerating into a battle of endurance: the Japanese had nowhere to withdraw to and the Americans had no room to manoeuvre. By the end of the second week over 13,000 Americans had been killed or injured but there would be no respite for the three divisions, the Marines continued to attack by day while the Japanese counter-attacked at night.

On 4 March the men fighting for Iwo Jima understood the significance of capturing the island when a damaged B29 Super Fortress called Dinah Might made an emergency landing on Airstrip One as it returned from a raid over Tokyo. After the crew had made repairs, cheers sent the huge plane on its way.

Fighting raged on for another twenty-two days, claiming another 11,000 American casualties, but the combined weight of firepower, hitting the Japanese positions from the air, sea and land was devastating. As artillery pieces pounded the hills, planes blew caves apart with 1,000lb bombs and rocket-armed landing craft targeted the cliffs along the shore. Although there was no doubt about the final outcome of the battle, every Japanese soldier was determined to exact a high price for his own life.

It took thirty-six days to subdue General Kuribayashi's men. Over 22,000 were killed and they had exacted a high price on V Amphibious Corps: General Schmidt's command had suffered over 24,000 casualties, the highest total for a single Marine Corps action.

With Mount Suribachi clear, General Schmidt could turn his attentions to the north of the island ready to attack with three divisions on 25 February. Landing craft continued to deliver men and supplies to the island and LSM 92 drops off another load of Amtracs.
(127-GW-112888)

Pole-charges, explosives strapped to a long handle, were found to be effective for knocking out bunkers. Men would have to work their way forward under covering fire until they were close enough to press the charge against the gun aperture. Private Dale Billings is putting the finishing touches to a charge before adding it to the pile.
(127-GW-112017)

Time for a smoke; Private Wilfred Voegeli stops for a minute in the midst of the smouldering ruins of a Japanese bunker complex. (127-GW-111147)

Guardian of the Skies. Fighter and attack squadrons bombed and strafed the island at every opportunity and the pilot of this Grumman F6F Hellcat is taking advantage of a clear sky during a dawn patrol. (127-GW-126222)

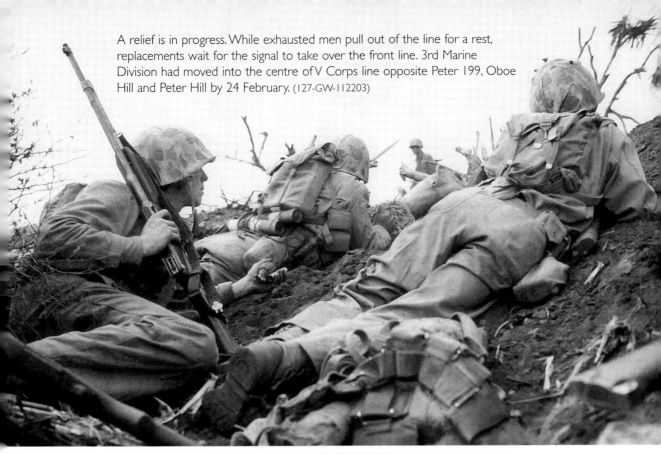

A relief is in progress. While exhausted men pull out of the line for a rest, replacements wait for the signal to take over the front line. 3rd Marine Division had moved into the centre of V Corps line opposite Peter 199, Oboe Hill and Peter Hill by 24 February. (127-GW-112203)

Meanwhile, on the west flank 5th Division had to clear Nishi Ridge before it could enter The Gorge. This young Marine still has scraps of waterproofing attached to the bayonet of his rifle. (127-GW-112202)

A combination of soft sand and rough terrain limited the areas where tanks could operate; and the Japanese usually had them covered with anti-tank guns. The leading tank had to be abandoned after it bogged down in a huge crater; the second one has lost a track. (127-GW-111039)

The lighter Amtracs could cope better with Iwo Jima's inhospitable landscape. Twin mounted machine gun turrets could keep snipers at bay while the crew ferried men and supplies around the island. (127-GW-109691)

4th Division fought day after day across the Meatgrinder, a series of rugged ridges and ravines known as Hill 382, the Amphitheatre, and the Turkey Knob, on the east coast of the island. As one Marine dodges forward to the next crater, the rest of his squad take a breather. (127-GW-112603)

3rd Division made V Corps' main attack towards Airstrip 2 covering the centre of the island. This Marine hugs the ground as another burst of machine gun fire targets Company L during 21st Regiment's drive towards the airfield. (127-GW-111389)

A Japanese sniper has been cornered and these three Marines are taking no chances, firing clip after clip of ammunition into the bunker. (127-GW-140752)

By 28 February, 3rd Division had reached the edge of Airstrip 2 and, although Japanese soldiers penetrated the Marines' front lines during night attacks, none survived. These two men have just helped clear the pillbox in the background and are now looking for their next objective. (127-GW-113803)

Inch by inch, yard by yard, the Marines worked their way across the northern part of Iwo Jima. This team is making sure that no one is left alive; two men cover the bunker aperture while a third squirts flaming fuel into the opening. (127-GW-111008)

Digging in for the night; Privates Madison Gross and Edwin Dimick keep a look out for snipers while Private Raymond Dirks swings the pick. The three men would take it in turn to dig the foxhole to spread the workload. (127-GW-112566)

Corporal Marlin Hoge pays little attention to a dead Japanese soldier as he scours the area for snipers. (127-GW-111967)

While the Marines pushed north towards Airstrip 2, work was underway to make Airstrip 1 functional. A transport plane flies low over the island, dropping essential supplies.
(127-GW-113041)

On 4 March, the first Boeing B-29 Super Fortress, Dinah Might, landed on Iwo Jima on its way back from a raid over Tokyo. It was the first sign of the island's significance in the bombing campaign on homeland Japan. After carrying out emergency repairs, the crew continued on their way. (127-GW-112392)

4 March marked the second week of the battle and although V Marine Corps held a line deep in the Japanese line, over 13,000 Marines had been killed or injured. This aerial view over Purple Beach shows the build up of troops and facilities on the south tip of the island. (111-SC-206876)

Avengers of a Marine torpedo bomber squadron escort transport planes to the island. (127-GW-121884)

As the Marines began to clear the high ground, observers were able to observe direct fire for ships offshore. 47th Fighter Squadron arrived on the island on 6 March and the pilots soon learnt how to fly their P-51 Mustangs in close support, using 1,000lb bombs to destroy fortifications. These Marines of 3rd Regiment have paused to watch the air show. (127-GW-178526)

Although the end result of the Iwo Jima campaign was never in doubt after 5 March, the battle would rage on for another twenty-two days and would claim an additional 11,000 American casualties and the lives of virtually the entire Japanese garrison. The crew of this 75mm howitzer are firing directly at a Japanese bunker. (127-GW-113644)

The Japanese troops usually fought defensively, taking advantage of the rough terrain and their comprehensive fortifications. On the night of 8 March, General Senda led a counter-attack against 4th Marine Division. The eight hundred strong force was wiped out in ferocious hand-to-hand fighting. These Marines of 23rd Regiment have fixed bayonets before moving out. (127-GW-142979)

Quick wits, a nerve of steel and a lot of luck were needed to survive. This squad has just scattered after a Japanese soldier tossed a grenade into their midst. The battle for the emplacement would continue when the dust has settled. (127-GW-114681)

The Marines needed to use every trick in the book to outwit a cunning enemy. This attempt to fool a sniper with a spare helmet failed to work. (127-GW-113649)

The rugged coastline was riddled with caves linked by an intricate network of tunnels and it would take days to clear them. Flamethrowers made sure no one was left alive in this cave before the engineers moved in with their explosives. (111-SC-208586)

As the battle grew to climax and the surviving Japanese troops were pushed into a corner, the fighting became more desperate. Having discovered a hidden bunker, these Marines hug the rocks for cover as one of their charges explodes in a mass of flames and smoke. (127-GW-114292)

Close fighting ensued in the gullies and ravines as the Marines cleared the caves along the north coast of the island. This man is giving directions to a machine gun crew from his hidden position so they can fire into the mouth of a cave. (127-GW-114027)

Tanks struggled to find suitable routes across the rough landscape but were always very welcome when they could find a way through. This squad pause while a Sherman clears a track with its dozer blade. (127-GW-114025)

Camouflaged anti-tank guns and hidden howitzers exacted their toll on the Marine tank crews. A random artillery shell hit the engine of this Sherman as it supported 5th Division's attack on the Gorge. The crew would have had little chance of escaping. (127-GW-112900)

All is not as it seems! The volcanic rock on Iwo Jima was soft enough to carve with a sharp knife and enterprising Japanese soldiers have sculpted a model of a tank in the hope of drawing fire from the their fortifications. (111-SC-208998)

Japanese tanks were designed to operate in jungle areas and much smaller and lighter than their American counterparts. The crew of this example had hidden their machine out of sight in the hope of catching Marines as they picked their way across a shallow ravine. (127-GW-143230)

After thirty-six days of savage fighting, Iwo Jima was finally cleared, and it was time to count the cost. Over 24,000 Marines were dead or wounded; the majority of the 22,000 Japanese had been killed. 2nd Battalion of 21st Regiment landed on D+2 and over the days that followed amassed a large armoury of captured weapons and equipment. (127-GW-113119)

15th Fighter Group had been providing air cover for the bombing raids on Tokyo since 6 March and, occasionally, damaged B29 Super-fortresses would land on Iwo Jima's narrow airstrip for repairs. Before long the island would become the centre of the bombing campaign against mainland Japan. (127-GW-115101)

Chapter Seven

L-Day on Okinawa and the capture of Motobu Peninsula

Okinawa stood at the gateway to Japan and since the summer of 1944, Japanese troops had been pouring onto the island to build fortifications in line with General Kuribayashi's plan to repel an invasion. By March 1945 they were ready and, as 77th Division cleared a number of outlying islands in preparation for the main assault, everyone realised that Operation ICEBERG was going to be a costly campaign.

On 1 April, Task Force 56, a fleet of ten battleships, nine cruisers, twenty-three destroyers and over one hundred rocket gunboats opened L-Day. It was the heaviest concentration of naval gunfire ever used during an amphibious invasion. As shells hit the shoreline, hundreds of landing craft and amphibious vehicles carried two infantry and two Marine divisions towards the Hagushi beaches on the western side of the island. Simulated amphibious landings off the southeast coast kept General Kuribayashi guessing and his decision to hold the interior of the island meant that Tenth Army was able to put over 60,000 men ashore by nightfall at the cost of a handful of casualties. It was the calm before the storm.

Advancing rapidly across the island, 7th Division reached the east coast the following day, followed by the 1st Marine Division, cutting Kuribayashi's forces in two. With the majority of General Kuribayashi's holding the fortified Shuri Line to the south, General Simon Buckner ordered the 6th Marine Division to drive north up the Ishikawa Isthmus while the rest of Tenth Army deployed. The marines moved quickly, finding the Japanese holding a mass of wooded ravines on the Motobu Peninsula. It would take over two weeks to eliminate organised resistance in the area.

While the American ground troops advanced across Okinawa, the Japanese Air Force struck, making kamikaze and conventional air attacks against Task Force 51's warships and landing craft. A final attempt to engage the American Navy on 6 April ended in disaster when the super battleship Yamato was spotted leaving Kyushu by a submarine; aircraft from Task Force 58's carriers intercepted the fleet and sank the pride of the Japanese Navy.

Meanwhile, XXIV Corps had deployed across the narrow waist of Okinawa north

Task Force 51 fired over 3,800 tons of shells at the island during the first 24 hours of Operation ICEBERG, forcing the Japanese to group their forces inland. This cruiser dwarfs the tiny landing craft carrying Marines to the northern beaches. (127-GW-116343)

of Shuri and Naha and on 5 April attacked the ridges and hills covering the Outer Shuri Line. For the next three days 96th Division fought on the slopes of Cactus Ridge while 7th Division battled to capture the Pinnacle. Targeted by mortars, artillery and machine guns, the GIs continued to advance onto Kakazu Ridge, where the Japanese were waiting in bunkers and tunnels. As the attacks stalled on the lower slopes, Japanese counter-attacks infiltrated the American lines but each time XXIV Corps line held. Inch-by-inch Buckner's men pushed forward into the Shuri Line in what was becoming a battle of endurance.

As the flotilla of warships bombarded Okinawa, Task Force 56, comprising hundreds of landing craft and amphibious personnel carriers, assembled off the coast. Scrambling down the side of the ships into the landing craft as they bobbed around in the choppy sea was a dangerous operation.
(CG 408293)

Marines cram into their LVT and prepare to make the run into the beach. Will it be another nightmare landing like the one on Iwo Jima or have the Japanese abandoned to shoreline?
(127-GW-116090)

Landing craft armed with rockets battered the shoreline during the final run into the beach.
(CG 408290)

At 04:00 hours Vice-Admiral Turner gave the order 'Land the Landing Force' and over the next four hours the huge flotilla of landing craft and amphibious vehicles formed up while Task Force 51 bombarded the beaches with shells and rockets, alternating with air attacks by Marine and Naval fighters.

Full speed ahead! The coastguard pilots open the throttle on their landing craft and forge through the surf towards the shore. Unlike previous operations, coral reefs did not affect General Buckner's plan for Operation ICEBERG.
(127-GW-116915)

These Alligators have been fitted with gun turrets and were ideal for supporting the infantry both on land and in the water. They have left their landing craft and are swimming through the choppy surf towards the beach. (127-GW-206509)

The might of the American Navy assembled off the coast had forced General Ushijima to concentrate his forces inland, leaving the beaches virtually undefended. Over 16,000 men were ashore within the hour and these Marines count themselves fortunate as they wade through the surf onto dry land. (127-GW-116368)

Ship based Navy Hellcats flew in low, looking for Japanese troops assembling to counter-attack the beachhead; they were usually disappointed (127-GW-116514)

The Memphis Belle hits the beach and the Marines waste no time jumping out into the surf on Blue Beach 2. General Buckner could rely on 1,700 LVTs, 300 of them armoured with turret mounted howitzers, and 700 DUKWs, amphibious trucks, to ferry his men ashore. (127-GW-117019)

Marines swarm over the seawall on Blue beach expecting to come under fire at any moment. Corporal James Day, a squad leader with the 22nd Marines could not believe his luck: *'I didn't hear a single shot all morning, it was unbelievable!'* (127-GW-116909)

Marines of the 6th Division swarmed across Yontan airfield within hours of landing. 7th Division also captured Kadena on L-Day and, within days, fighter planes were able to operate from the island.
(127-GW-116108)

After a successful landing on Blue Beach, Marines of the 6th Division regroup and prepare to move inland. By nightfall over 60,000 men were ashore. Casualties were less than two hundred, a fraction of what had been expected. (127-GW-116911)

Everyone had predicted heavy losses in the first few hours but the landing had proved to be an easy victory. It was, however, only the start of a gruelling three-month long campaign. Marines move out accompanied by Sherman tanks and Alligators. (127-GW-116424)

This aerial view of the landing beaches illustrates the massive logistical flotilla supporting Tenth Army. Tiny landing craft ferry troops from the landing ships to the beach while amphibious vehicles carry supplies and equipment ashore. Meanwhile, destroyers keep a watchful eye for Japanese Kamikaze planes.

The build up of troops was rapid and Army and Marine troops pushed inland quickly to where 32nd Army were waiting in fortified zones covering the central and southern highlands. General Ushijima intended to draw General Buckner's troops away from their naval support while the Japanese Air Force took on the American Navy. (111-SC-269177)

The Japanese Air Force struck back at the American Fleet anchored off Okinawa on 6 April and, while fighters and bombers carried out conventional attacks, kamikaze planes tried to crash their planes into Vice Admiral Turner's ships. The sky is dotted with anti-aircraft fire as a pilot aims his burning plane towards an aircraft carrier.

Over 2,300 kamikaze missions were flown during the battle of Okinawa and, although many pilots never made it to their objective, Fifth Fleet lost 34 ships and another 368 were damaged. Over 9,000 Naval personnel were killed or injured. This pilot has made it through the screen of fighters and anti-aircraft fire to fulfil his dream of flying his plane into an American ship.

Marine Corsair Fighter Planes return to base after another successful sortie.
(127-GW-78262)

Both 7th Division and 1st Marine Division made rapid advances across the narrow waist of Okinawa and by the afternoon of 2 April, the island had been cut in half. The crew of this LVT is waiting for an opportunity to use its 75mm Howitzer as it moves across the island. (127-GW-119270)

96th Deadeye Division advanced so quickly, as it moved across central Okinawa towards Cactus Ridge, that it outran its supply line. Fighter-bombers were used to drop badly needed ammunition, rations and medical supplies to help keep Major-General James Bradley's men moving. (111-SC-207972)

In the north 6th Marine Division moved rapidly up the Ishikawa Isthmus capturing Nago, the largest town in northern Okinawa on 7 April. 22nd Regiment travelled on top of tanks and self-propelled guns driving the Japanese before them. (127-GW-116705)

Japanese rearguards were swept aside during the advance to Nago and this squad of Marines keep moving after killing a sniper. (127-GW-119485)

But the honeymoon period was about to end. 6th Marine Division found the Kunigami Detachment concentrated on the Motobu Peninsula in an area called Yae-Take. The Marines had to fight their way across a maze of ravines and ridges to dig the Japanese soldiers out of their caves. (127-GW-116527)

Private Stephen Ferraro, a veteran of three Pacific campaigns, calls his demolition team forward to destroy a fortified cave.
(127-GW-118307)

War-dog platoons were used to search the cave systems in Yae-Take. Their leader, Lieutenant Crankshaw, was leading his Reconnaissance Platoon when a Japanese sniper tried his luck.
(127-GW-118780)

Motobu Peninsula area was finally cleared on 20 April. No prisoners were taken. Colonel Udo and his Detachment died to a man. 6th Marine Division had suffered over 950 casualties clearing the northern part of Okinawa, its first battle. (127-GW-112067)

While the Marines cleared the northern part of the island, XIV Army Corps had been wheeling into line opposite the Shuri Line, General Ushijima's main line of fortifications. Machine gun fire is preventing these engineers from clearing a path through a minefield on 96th Division's front; the tank has resorted to blowing a way through with its own guns. (111-SC-204284)

The battle in the south started on 5 April with 96th and 7th Division attacking Cactus Ridge and the Pinnacle, a series of low hills covering the Shuri Line. 749th Field Artillery Battalion fires its huge eight-inch Howitzers at the Japanese lines, the first time these fearsome weapons had been used in the Pacific. (111-SC-207316)

Rockets away! Over 700 Marine planes gave close support to the ground troops during the battle for Okinawa and the pilot of this Corsair has just released his eight five-inch rockets against suspected enemy positions. The salvo was the equivalent to a destroyer's broadside and the concussion from the blast nearly caused the photographer's plane to crash. (127-GW-129356)

The Japanese artillery and mortars were well hidden on the hills in front of the Outer Shuri Line and snipers made sure that the GIs kept under cover as often as possible. This patrol is moving forward to find a suitable observation post. (111-SC-207300)

Over the next four days and nights XIV Corps inched their way onto the ridges knowing full well that the Japanese had intimate knowledge of the ground. Here a machine gun crew of 96th Division are giving covering fire as a platoon edges towards a Japanese bunker on Cactus Ridge. (111-SC-207321)

The Japanese were not on the island of Okinawa; they were in it, hiding in an intricate system of caves and tunnels. While flame-throwing Sherman tanks squirt burning fluid into a series of caves along Kakazu Ridge, GIs wait for the signal to move forward and mop up. (111-SC-208302)

The outpost hills were cleared by 8 April and XIV Corps had suffered over 1,500 casualties while Japanese losses were estimated at three times that number. Medics were often targeted by snipers in the hope of drawing more men into an area. This group are struggling to evacuate their casualty across broken ground. (111-SC-207309)

The island was covered in hundreds of family tombs and each one was a potential hiding place. Two dead snipers were found at the entrance of this smoking mausoleum following a mortar barrage. Another three were coaxed out alive after more explosives had been used.
(111-SC-206508)

Two war-dog trainers rest their animals, sheltered by an Okinawan tomb. The dogs had been trained to search underground bunkers for snipers. (111-SC-206500)

While XIV Corps pushed south onto Kakazu Ridge, mopping operations continued across the island. Working under enemy machine gun and mortar fire, engineers throw a second charge into the mouth of a cave while a Marine watches to see if anyone emerges after the dust has cleared. (127-GW-120062)

There would be no respite on Kakazu Ridge. Night after night General Ushijima's launched suicidal counterattacks against the American line. These exhausted men take advantage of the morning sun to grab a few minutes rest. (127-GW-123065)

Chapter Eight

The Battle for the Shuri Line

The clearing of Motobu Peninsula allowed 77th Division to land on the island of Ie Shima off the northwest coast of Okinawa on 16 April and after a week of heavy fighting on the Pinnacle and Legusugu Mountain the garrison was eliminated. US engineers moved ashore and built an airstrip turning the island into an ideal base for air attacks against targets on Okinawa.

On the mainland, XXIV Corps was still struggling to make progress into the Outer Shuri Line and even the addition of an extra division to the American line had made little difference to the Japanese defenders. General Buckner's men renewed the attack against Kakazu Ridge on 19 April, relying on the firepower from eighteen warships, 300 artillery pieces and 650 planes to pave the way. The effects were negligible and the Japanese emerged from deep caves to fight as soon as the bombardment had ended. They ended Buckner's hopes for a rapid armoured thrust over the ridge, destroying twenty-two American tanks in a few hours. The GIs would have to rely on explosives and flamethrowers to burn or blast their enemies out of their bunkers on Skyline Ridge and Tombstone Ridge. General Buckner would later refer to these new tactics as the *'blowtorch and corkscrew'* method.

Ernie Pyle, a popular war correspondent who was known as the GIs' buddy, was killed on Ie Shima. 77th Division erected this memorial on the spot where he was hit by a Japanese machine gun. (111-SC-206490)

Progress was slow and costly, but one by one, the hills and ridges of the Outer Shuri Line fell as April came to a close. 27th Division had reached the summit of Urasoe-Mura Escarpment and while 7th Division advanced onto Hill 178, 96th Division was not far behind, clearing Tanabaru Escarpment and Nishibaru Ridge in the centre of XXIV Corps line. Having forced a way through the first line of the Japanese defences, XXIV Corps reorganised just in time to meet General Ushijima's counterattack on 4 May. As 32nd Army's infantry, tanks and artillery fought to regain

As soon as the Marines had cleared Motobu Peninsula, 77th Division landed on the island of Ie Shima on 16 April where there was heavy fighting on Bloody Ridge and Iegusugu Mountain. Infantry take cover alongside an M8 self-propelled howitzer while planes fly low overhead to bomb the Japanese positions. (111-SC-206488)

the Outer Shuri Line, kamikaze aircraft and boats attacked the American supply lines and shipping, sinking seventeen ships. Although the Japanese pushed XXIV Corps back a short distance, their casualties had been enormous and as 7th Division struck back, clearing Maeda Escarpment on 7 May, General Ushijima had to admit that it was only a matter of time before Okinawa fell to the Americans.

General Buckner renewed the attack against the Inner Shuri Line on 11 May and while the Marines battled across Dakeshi and Wana Ridges and up the slopes of the Sugar Loaf. GIs fought and died on hills with names such as the Chocolate Drop, the Wart and Flattop. The first breakthrough came two days later when 96th Division captured Conical Hill on the east coast. However, heavy rains prevented the rest of XXIV Corps moving forward and over the days that followed, thousands of Japanese troops abandoned the ruins of Shuri and Naha and withdrew to a new defensive line on the Yaeju-Dake Escarpment at the south end of the island.

While the rest of XXIV Corps pushed forward, 6th Marine Division landed on the north coast of the Oroku Peninsula, bypassing the main Japanese line. The move made little difference and as American casualties soared to over 35,000 (including General Buckner), General Ushijima refused to surrender, choosing to commit ritual suicide on 22 June. The loss of 32nd Army's leader heralded the end of organised resistance on Okinawa and as hundreds of Japanese soldiers followed their leader's example rather than surrender. XXIV Corps cleared out the last pockets of resistance. America's bloodiest campaign in the Pacific finally came to an end on 2 July 1945.

The assault on the Outer Shuri Line began on 19 April and it was heralded by the largest concentration of firepower in the Pacific campaign, eighteen war ships and over three hundred artillery pieces. (127-GW-120807)

Over 650 Navy and Marine planes strafed and dive-bombed Kakazu Ridge, Nishibaru Ridge, and Tanabaru Escarpment before XXIV Corps attacked. The combined effects of the air, sea and land barrage had been negligible. The Japanese were able to take cover in a network of tunnels and caves. (127-GW-126465)

An armoured attack on Kakazu reach was repulsed with heavy losses when the tanks became separated from their infantry scouts. Twenty-two were destroyed in a few hours. An M18 tank destroyer of 306th Anti-tank Company engages a bunker at close range during the battle for Maeda escarpment. (111-SC-208054)

Heavy fighting continued but, one by one, the Japanese positions around Item Pocket and on Kochi Ridge and Urasoe-Mura Escarpment were cleared. Flamethrower tanks and small demolition crews worked side-by-side to clear out the bunkers and caves using what General Buckner referred to as *'blowtorch and corkscrew'* methods. (111-SC-208096)

The capture of Maeda escarpment on 7 May unhinged the Shuri defence line and as General Ushijima launched desperate counter-attacks, Marines and GIs fought off suicidal charges by Japanese infantry and tanks. (127-GW-123329)

Meanwhile, 1st Marine Division fought its way up the slopes of the Sugar Loaf. The men of 29th Regiment's 1st Battalion dig in for the night as the artillery continues to pound the summit of the hill. Three days after this photograph was taken a shell hit an observation post as Major Thomas Myers briefed his company commanders. The explosion killed Myers and wounded every officer present. (127-GW-121365)

A bazooka team inch their way up a slope towards a bunker while the rest of the squad give covering fire. After securing the Sugar Loaf, on 18 May the Marines captured the Half Moon and the Horseshoe. Shuri ridge, overlooking the island's capital was next.
(127-GW-122617)

While the GIs up front call for support, their radioman relays the fall of shot to the crew of an M7 Priest self-propelled howitzer. Close cooperation between the mobile artillery and the infantry was particularly important to ensure accurate fire during counter-attacks, many of which took place at night.
(127-GW-122036)

Soldiers of 96th Division use a 37mm anti-tank gun to blast apart a pillbox. The GIs found that they could wheel the lightweight weapon over the rough terrain as the hills along the east coast, named Dick, Oboe, and Conical Hill, were captured one by one.
(111-SC-208587)

Marines follow at a safe distance as flame throwing tanks target bunkers on the crest of a ridge. With both the Sugar Loaf and Conical Hill in American hands, the flanks of the Shuri Line were lost and General Ushijima ordered a general withdrawal on to the Kiyamu Peninsula (127-GW-120369)

6th Marine Division began to cross the rain-swollen Asato River on 23 May and entered Naha on the west coast, finding large parts of the town deserted. Marine snipers played cat-and-mouse with their Japanese counterparts for several days. (127-GW-123203)

These marines have cornered a sniper in a ruined building and while two men give covering fire, the third throws a smoke grenade. It took several days to clear the mined town. (127-GW-123324)

Although Shuri Castle was in 77th Division's zone, the Japanese had evacuated the ridge overlooking the town, allowing 1st Marine Division to reach the ruins on 29 May. A company commander from South Carolina erected the Confederate Stars and Bars flag much to the annoyance of Yankee Marines and soldiers in the area, prompting a host of angry calls to Major-General Pedro del Valle's headquarters. It was two days before Lieutenant-Colonel Richard Ross could reach the castle with the Stars and Stripes. (127-GW-121833)

Shuri town had also been abandoned but buildings such as this church made an ideal snipers nest. A patrol circles around to the rear of the building while the men in the foreground give covering fire. (127-GW-123171)

While the main fighting line moved further south, patrols had to keep watch in both Shuri and Naha in case Japanese soldiers emerged from their hiding places to carry out suicide attacks on the American supply columns. (127-GW-122941)

Marines of 22nd Regiment cautiously enter a tomb that had been used as an ammunition store. The tombs were linked by an intricate maze of tunnels that allowed General Ushijima's men to shelter from the American bombardments. (127-GW-122506)

It took several days to clear the ring of tunnels and bunkers covering Naha. After dropping an explosive charge into one bunker, Marines wait with their rifles at the ready in case anyone tries to escape. Japanese soldiers sometimes strapped explosives to themselves before they emerged, in the hope of killing American soldiers as they committed suicide. (127-GW-120053)

Tenth Army missed the opportunity to corner the main body of General Ushijima's 32nd Army as it slipped away onto the Kiyamu Peninsula and rearguards kept the Americans at bay while heavy rain and deep mud threatened to stall the advance. Snipers have pinned these Marines down behind the tombstones on Cemetery Ridge. (127-GW-122639)

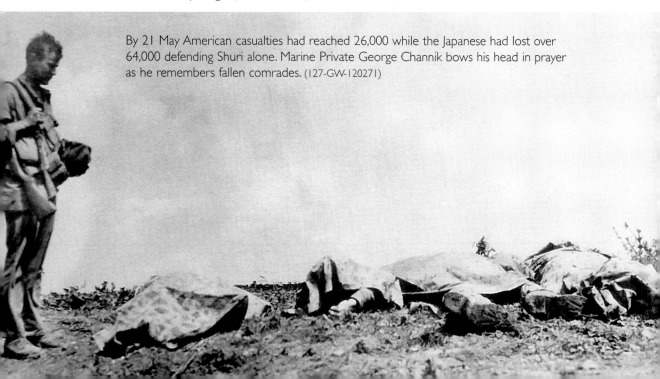

By 21 May American casualties had reached 26,000 while the Japanese had lost over 64,000 defending Shuri alone. Marine Private George Channik bows his head in prayer as he remembers fallen comrades. (127-GW-120271)

Japanese *Sally* bombers loaded with *Giretsu*, Japanese commandos, tried to land on the Yontan landing strip in an attempt to wreak havoc across the US airbase. Most of the planes were shot down by anti-aircraft guns, but this one managed to reach the runway. Over twenty American planes were damaged and thousands of gallons of aviation fuel were torched before the raiders were killed. The suicidal attack made little difference. (127-GW-208461)

The rains came down at the end of May and advances could be measured in metres as heavy rains turned the battlefield into a quagmire. These lorries loaded with supplies for the front are waiting to be towed out by bulldozers. (127-GW-208608)

Tenth Army fired over two million rounds, while ships off shore expended over 700,00 rockets and shells during the battle for Okinawa. The crew of this 105mm howitzer are providing support for 6th Marine Division following its amphibious assault on the Oroku Peninsula, south of Naha. (127-GW-123533)

A Sherman moves forward to support 1st Marine Division's attack on Wana Gorge, a narrow ravine riddled with caves and surrounded by towering cliffs. 1st Tank Battalion expended 5,000 rounds of 75mm, 173,000 rounds of .30-caliber ammunition, and over 600 gallons of napalm on 16 May alone. (127-GW-124263)

A new weapon appeared on the battlefield in June, the 57mm recoilless rifle. The lightweight anti-tank gun was extremely useful for knocking out bunkers and this example was used to support 96th Division's attack on Yaeju-Dake Escarpment. (111-SC-208426)

7th Division began their assault on Yaeju-Dake Escarpment on the night of 12 June and before long the whole ridgeline was under attack. Rain and mud had plagued the attack and during one report, 96th Division stated that the men on the forward slope slid down while those on reverse slope slid back. This Marine returns fire as he crawls forward. (127-GW-122608)

Demolition teams worked their way across the peninsula looking for bunkers and tunnel entrances. Usually they took no chances and used a variety of methods to clear them out. This Marine is making sure he throws his satchel charge to the back of a dugout on Hill 69. (127-GW-124269)

Two Marines drop phosphorus grenades into a cave after sealing the entrance. If the explosion did not kill anyone inside, the poisonous fumes would finish them off. (127-GW-124583)

The flamethrower could spray burning fuel deep into the tunnels with the help of a high-pressure tank and nozzle. Snipers made it their priority to try and take out any man carrying the fearsome weapon. (127-GW-127958)

Although General Buckner sent a note to General Ushijima, urging him to surrender, 32nd Army's commander had no intention of being taken alive. As Shermans of 769th Tank Battalion led 96th Division's attack on the high peaks of the Yaeju-Dake Escarpment, the Japanese General committed ritual suicide, *seppuku*, on 22 June. Buckner had been killed in action four days earlier. (111-SC-209658)

Other strongholds fell one by one as resistance began to disintegrate. Hundreds of Japanese soldiers chose to follow their leaders example, and many tried to kill American soldiers with grenades or explosives as they committed suicide. 6th Marine Division cleared a number of smaller islands off the coast of Okinawa during the final stages of the campaign and the men of 2nd Battalion give a big cheer as they raise the Stars on Stripes on Senaga Shima. (127-GW-125052

Organised resistance had virtually ended by the evening of 21 June but Tenth Army had suffered over 8,000 casualties since the fall of Shuri, testimony to the fierce fighting on Yaeju-Dake Escarpment. (127-GW-119484)

Over 100,000 Japanese soldiers remained at large on Okinawa until the end of the war. Military police keep a close watch on this group while they wait their turn to be interrogated. (111-SC-209885)

The site of a Japanese shrine is the perfect place for a writing table. I have survived the savage fighting on Okinawa would be a common theme in letters to loved ones back home.
(127-GW-123551)

Marine Lieutenant Sol Mayer, the fighting mess officer of Major George Axtell's Death Rattler fighter squadron, inspects a samurai sword he has just acquired. Mayer swapped steaks, chops and ice cream with the ground troops in exchange for souvenirs to pass round the Marine pilots.(127-GW-124053)

A Japanese suicide plane stands idly at Yontan airfield. *'The suicide plane is a very effective weapon which we must not underestimate'* reported Admiral Spruance. He spoke from personal experience. Kamikaze planes knocked out his first flagship, the heavy cruiser *Indianapolis*, and severely damaged the battleship *New Mexico*. (127-GW-120791)

Organised resistance collapsed at the end of June but mopping up opertions continued for another two months. Many Japanese soldiers hid in the caves along the coastline and refused to surrender. Hundreds committed suicide but many others had to be hunted down. Flame throwing tanks and engineers worked side by side to clear out possible hiding places. (111-SC-210416)

Chapter Nine

The Surrender of Japan

Even though the campaigns to liberate the Philippines and Okinawa came to an end at the beginning of July, thousands of Japanese soldiers were still holding out in the mountains and jungles hoping for a change in fortunes. After the horrendous losses on Okinawa, the prospect of an amphibious assault on mainland Japan was a daunting prospect and as the Soviet Army planned to intervene in the war against Japan, America's new President, Harry S Truman, wanted a speedy conclusion to the war in the Pacific.

One possible solution was provided on 16 July. For some time the Allies had been striving to harness nuclear energy and the successful testing of an atomic weapon at Alamogordo gave the American President the answer, albeit a terrifying one. The Potsdam Declaration of 26 July, calling for Japan's immediate and unconditional surrender, was made with the knowledge that atomic weapons could be unleashed. The Japanese High Command refused, setting the scene for the dawning of a new age of warfare.

On the morning of 6 August *Enola Gay*, a B29 Superfortress piloted by Colonel Paul Tibbets, flew over the port of Hiroshima at the southern end of the Japanese mainland. It dropped a single bomb codenamed *Little Boy* and as Tibbets turned his plane for home, the bomb exploded at two thousand feet. *'A bright light filled the plane, we turned back to look at Hiroshima. The city was hidden by that awful cloud...boiling up, mushrooming'.*

The blast burnt everything in its path and the strong winds generated by the shock wave demolished virtually everything within a three-kilometre radius of the explosion. Thousands were immediately killed or seriously injured but worse was to come; radiation sickness affected many of the survivors and estimates put the death toll over the first twelve months at more than 140,000.

Three days later a second atomic bomb, codenamed *Fat Man,* was dropped on the nearby city of Nagasaki, killing thousands in the initial blast. Thousands more died of their injuries and from radiation sickness in the years that followed and the legacy of atomic warfare affected many more for generations.

While the Japanese Supreme War Council considered the Allies demands to surrender, some commanders were determined to defend their homeland to the end in a quest for victory or annihilation. Emperor Hirohito's unprecedented broadcast to the nation called for his people to bear the unbearable and on 28 August, Allied warships sailed into Tokyo harbour to prepare for the formal surrender of Imperial Japan.

Following the German capitulation, thousands of GIs across Europe were waiting to be redeployed to the Pacific Theatre and the news of the Japanese surrender was met with a mixture of joy and relief. They would be going home soon. English girls join American soldiers as they parade the Stars and Stripes through the streets of London. (111-SC-210353)

Thousands of Japanese troops continued to hold out in the hills on Okinawa, Luzon and other small islands across the Pacific. Many had no means of communication and rather than risk lives by sending GIs into the jungle, loudspeakers were used while planes dropped leaflets. Weather balloons adorned with banners announcing the surrender were tried in 38th Division's area on Luzon. (111-SC-262859)

The mushroom cloud of the atomic bomb, dropped on the shipbuilding centre of Nagasaki.

On the morning of 2 September General Douglas MacArthur met the Japanese envoys on the deck of the USS *Missouri* and at four minutes past nine o'clock the war in the Pacific came to an end. The General announced the news to the world with the following words:

'Today the guns are silent. A great tragedy has ended.
A great victory has been won...'

Three weeks after the two atom bombs had been dropped on mainland Japan, General MacArthur landed at Atsugi Airport ready to sign the formal surrender documents. (111-SC-210613)

The formal surrender ceremony was held on 31 August on the deck of USS Missouri which had been anchored in Tokyo Bay. General MacArthur signs the papers while Lieutenant-General Jonathan Wainwright, commander of the Philippine forces, and Lieutenant-General Percival, British commander of the British troops in Singapore look on. Both commanders had been forced to surrender their commands in 1942 and had endured terrible hardships at the hands of their Japanese guards. (111-SC-210625)

Japanese politicians and generals gather on the deck of USS *Missouri* in front of the crowds as they wait to sign the surrender papers. (111-SC-210626)

A dejected General Yamashita waits to sign the surrender of Japanese forces in the Philippines. The defiant General refused to sign the papers until the day after the ceremony on USS *Missouri*. (111-SC-263531)

All across the Philippines thousands of Japanese prisoners of war were put to work repairing the damage they had caused to the towns and cities. The letters PW clearly stand out on the backs of these prisoners as they march through Manila and prepare to start another day's work clearing debris from the streets.
(111-SC-264172)

All across the islands of the Pacific cemeteries, large and small, were filled with the graves of young men who would not be going home. Over 11,000 GIs were killed in the Philippines campaign; more than 6,000 Marines perished on Iwo Jima, and the British, Indian and ANZAC troops suffered equally; another 12,500 were killed on Okinawa. Thousands more were injured or struck down by disease. Japanese losses were considerably higher.
(111-SC-209884)